RHIANNON CREE KIRSHNER

BEST OF LUCK

955 INFINITE LAYERS OF THE SOUL

PART 1

Best of Luck
955 INFINITE LAYERS OF THE SOUL
PART 1

iUniverse books may be ordered through booksellers or by contacting:

iUniverse
1663 Liberty Drive
Bloomington, IN 47403
www.iuniverse.com
1-800-Authors (1-800-288-4677)

Because of the dynamic nature of the Internet, any web addresses or links contained in this book may have changed since publication and may no longer be valid. The views expressed in this work are solely those of the author and do not necessarily reflect the views of the publisher, and the publisher hereby disclaims any responsibility for them.

ISBN: 978-1-5320-3932-4 (sc)
ISBN: 978-1-5320-3933-1 (e)
ISBN: 978-1-5320-3931-7 (hc)

Library of Congress Control Number: 2018901953

Print information available on the last page.

iUniverse rev. date: 08/28/2018

Dedication

Maybe I write for my family of friends and guides, Garrett P, Rebecca, Nate, Kayla, Isaac, Unique, Crystal, Bobby, Morgan, Tre Carter, West, Miles, the Brandon's, Virginia Newman, V, the Richard's, the Nicole's, Tyler's, Mathew's, and the David's, RED, Patrick, Pete, Luke, Alan, Anthony, Jeremy, Ruby, Bryan, the John's, Leslie, Paige, Gabe, Dustin, Ernesto, Morgan, Emi, Tiffany, Sebastian, Jeremy, Billy-Joe, Steve and Bear, Elijah, Ana B, Jessica H, Martin, Christopher, Mary Beth, my family and the multitude of others who have taken my soul to new heights and supported me every step of the way as genuine friends. They saw me and loved me for all I brought into their lives and vice versa. These are the people who I want most to see what I've made in their honor, to always have a piece of me to hold, as they hold me in their hearts, and have always set me free as the spirit to be all I can be. They are my destiny friends, people I will carry with me and cherish throughout my life, the infinite ones. Know that I felt this in all of my being as this was written.

Introduction

FLIP A COIN

Tails Up

I see the web that is spun for me and how every word symbolizes a piece of time aligning on each thread. The words "Best of Luck" are weaved along a sacred vibration drawing me back to the first moment when I read that phrase inscribed on a napkin, a napkin embroidered with a rose, signed by a celebrity who encouraged my skill as he handed me back the pen. I felt empowered to tell the tale of luck and how it always circles back to my initial drawing boards. As a young girl with that pen and that phrase, I went home and sat at my art desk writing out every loving desire I held onto tiny slips of paper, then I put them into a dream box and sealed it away. Ten years later I found that box and opened it, taking out each slip of paper and reading it one by one. I discovered that each word met it's peace - brought to manifest with the passing of time within that box.

Every word is a possibility waiting to emerge into the world. A possible truth and a possible journey. Stories don't just end when you put down the pen, they keep evolving. They keep resorting to the spaces where you aren't looking. The spaces where luck is found. They take shape in the canvas of your imagination as they take shape in your life.

I decided to cut right into the internal source of penmanship and define for myself the power of the craft. Choosing to go the distance in my mind I came back from an ever shifting reality with an answer to the strategic challenge of how to face adversity. Pick up that pen and set time in motion.

The challenge? Step out of your own way and let your heart reveal its voice.

Here I give you 955 reflections of my spirit to help guide you to that one thing you're looking for. That one thing that is looking for you within the vast layers that unfold to encompass the human soul. We may just be a small group of people doing a boundless amount of creative things, living each day to tell a new tale, give rise to reason, the up and coming, and spiritual introspection. With the "Tails Up", be the sacred anomaly that you are, write. Let your hands be your infinite guide. We are a movement of possibilities!

Heads Up

Those I met that served as guides to these words set me on a journey, leading me with a trail of pennies. I traded information with each of them of what attaches us to the source. A code of contact that uniquely weaves us into a dimensional grid of human relativity. To each a messenger.

I have written this book of a three year journey since my diagnosis of bipolar disorder that had me filling notebook to notebook with streams of rapid consciousness, only to come back with a note from the past that alerted many routes of possibility in the future. The words are a curious program that have greeted you here.There's a period after every perfect sentence, but an alignment of periods within every letter, every marking, and word.

Every letter is a crack to explore and dig through it's wreckage, for one letter contains a fallen nation. One by one by one. Follow the worst that is washed away, leaving only a smear to say we were here.

Best of luck. It is both a wish and a chance given to you in one simple phrase. What do you wish to find in these pages? What will you receive by chance that will you why the words were written for you now and not earlier? What are we approaching in our future that we'll choose to take with us? If you believe in your key, your token, then every line is a destination and every word an introduction.

The call of imagination is written courage...written hope. I'm not the only person with this in mind. I'm not the only person who comes back to rewind. We're stepping on sand that's not sinking and telling one another just to imagine that it is. Dip into this book spontaneously. Let your hands guide you to a wild card as you flip to the right first page- for you.

With the "Head's Up," help me create a daydream. With so many possible solutions to the equation of luck, we are bound to touch the same penny. Be as brave as you are...begin.

1. Maybe I write to separate from the stories of my past. I told you so much in one night. I painted myself by my accomplishments, when I meant to paint the picture of where they will lead.

2. Maybe I write because I respond to the intensity.

3. Maybe I write to defeat a system of delusions.

4. Maybe I write because I see life as it exists beyond the immediacy of the physical, but in a spiritual reality.

5. Maybe I write to relinquish shards of fear and anxiety that lurk in the shadows of the mind, for both thrive on ignorance.

6. Maybe I write to search, witness, question, and call on the source.

7. Maybe I write immersing in senses deep within the water hole of introspection.

8. Maybe I write, for it is the finest of garments in the plethora of fabrics in my life.

9. Maybe I write to learn from those around me who feel pushed into a rebellion.

10. Maybe I write for the lucky penny lingering around every corner.

11. Maybe I write with the courage not to think twice or harbor doubt.

12. Maybe I write because my soul has been sparked to chatter.

13. Maybe I write to draw upon the reservoir of commitment and determination.

14. Maybe I write for the paths we choose. There is quite the journey awaiting us all if you dare to venture. We are passengers on this soul trip.

15. Maybe I write for the component of me that only exists within your presence.

16. Maybe I write with the need to identify and an ideal to create.

17. Maybe I write to have clarity, serenity, and contentment in my days.

18. Maybe I write born from the vision of the first floating micro piece of light in a universe—thought.

19. Maybe I write to be free from conventional associations.

20. Maybe I write for the celebrations cloaked in myth and mystery.

21. Maybe I write because I've seen the glimmer set before everlasting hope.

22. Maybe I write to never feel like I am abandoning myself or the call to create.

23. Maybe I write to see you when it's my turn.

24. Maybe I write so I may never surrender my spirit.

25. Maybe I write to know luxury as a mind-set.

26. Maybe I write because an empty journal leaves me feeling like a phantom.

27. Maybe I write for the life that is folding in.

28. Maybe I write compatible to my surroundings.

29. Maybe I write for it is synonymous with both challenge and relief.

30. Maybe I write for the students of the way, the principled business folk, the timeless, and the lone wolf thinkers.

31. Maybe I write to refine my vision and enter the realm of the marvelous.

32. Maybe I write to meet you in the most peculiar of places.

33. Maybe I write for the greatness in the people I know and love. I needn't look far to find it, just through.

34. Maybe I write because it is the best alibi.

35. Maybe I write to be challenged to feel things I've never felt, dream things I've never dreamed, and move toward goals that once seemed unreachable.

36. Maybe I write to flood through emotional dimensions.

37. Maybe I write in light of the vast expansion of morality.

38. Maybe I write in love with the wealth of talk and storytelling.

39. Maybe I write for the symbols, patterns, and divination I am met by along the way.

40. Maybe I write to make the boldest decisions in my youth.

41. Maybe I write with the promise that one day I will truly have a platform to look back and say, "This is where I stand."

42. Maybe I write for the sensation of goosebumps.

43. Maybe I write to prevail, make possible, and rise to the occasion.

44. Maybe I write for all the "congratulations," "best wishes," "good lucks," "I am proud of you," "don't give up," and "you inspire me" messages.

45. Maybe I write seeing through your eyes, listening through your ears, and aligning with your instincts.

46. Maybe I write believing every friend I've ever made, road I've traveled down, hardship I've endured, and place I've planted my faith, to be a right one.

47. Maybe I write to reform the boundaries I once thought to exist around creativity.

48. Maybe I write for all the days that have gone by where I've said to myself, "Man, if I were to record that. " Well, here's to recording.

49. Maybe I write to the stranger whose gentle and inviting expressions gave me the notion to proclaim, "I love you."

50. Maybe I write to reach the summit just to smile.

51. Maybe I write to convey what I've been thinking, what I've known all along.

52. Maybe I write to file myself neatly, stoically away for future generations to uncover.

53. Maybe I write as I see angels appear in the people I meet, the places I go, the circumstances I find myself in, the behaviors I am witness to, and all that breathes and grows within the heart center.

54. Maybe I write only to face away from the sun's flashes, to preserve my eyes and improve their intricacy, capturing light that emanates from my essence.

55. Maybe I write to turn the pages, free the soul, and dance with the commanding forces.

56. Maybe I write to account for my every action and inaction, as the ultimate witness.

57. Maybe I write to assess the caliber of truth I've uncovered.

58. Maybe I write to analyze competing viewpoints and go the greater length in considering the one of strength and wisdom.

59. Maybe I write following a melody, fixed as time.

60. Maybe I write to the sky, for it carries the message. Always look up to receive.

61. Maybe I write to fill the cracks that turn the tables.

62. Maybe I write to share from experience.

63. Maybe I write where truth and fiction meet.

64. Maybe I write with the moral obligation to speak openly from the heart.

65. Maybe I write because it means so much to me to come into my thoughts for a good reason.

66. Maybe I write to be the seer and the subject.

67. Maybe I write to compensate for the answers no one cared to respond or expand upon.

68. Maybe I write working on the frontier of knowledge, paving over ignorance.

69. Maybe I write because I'm drawn to the page like a moth to a flame.

70. Maybe I write to set a stage for forms to take their mark.

71. Maybe I write for dreams to be an infinite blessing and wishes to never run out.

72. Maybe I write to knit a golden stitch.

73. Maybe I write to share a form of existence, a beating vibration that keeps me warm and secure, with each stroke of hand.

74. Maybe I write with a leveled comprehension of literature, good taste, and creative touch.

75. Maybe I write to roam freely in a living, thriving paradise, seen through kaleidoscope eyes.

76. Maybe I write to create what is worthy of me.

77. Maybe I write for the man I dressed in gold, and set the match for him to exist in form, as the impossible dream.

78. Maybe I write for the young, wise, pure souls who see the greatest adventure outside all means of fear.

79. Maybe I write to learn of my divinity, a power within us all.

80. Maybe I write to greet satisfaction where I stand and feel appreciation for it.

81. Maybe I write to shape a rebirth of inconceivable proportions.

82. Maybe I write to choose for myself what to focus on and believe in.

83. Maybe I write to cool away any foolish pride.

84. Maybe I write with the humble vision to embrace life by embracing what is given.

85. Maybe I write to attract through my dominant thoughts.

86. Maybe I write to fulfill my time with soul-fed work.

87. Maybe I write for hymns that vibrate like hummingbird wings.

88. Maybe I write beyond trivial affairs, for true good fortune.

89. Maybe I write to play with the present tense, instead of wrestling with the past.

90. Maybe I write to support a vocal revolution.

91. Maybe I write to uncover what it means to be an artist in this day in time.

92. Maybe I write for both victory and defeat.

93. Maybe I write to give myself an affirmation when conditions seem troubling.

94. Maybe I write for all the fast-approaching and inescapable possibilities I drummed up for my tomorrows.

95. Maybe I write for the destination it has given me.

96. Maybe I write because in the raging currents of time, there is no place for silence.

97. Maybe I write of a curious mind filled with innovative light and love energy.

98. Maybe I write to find love and glory in the imperfections of my evolution.

99. Maybe I write as a pen pal with the universe.

100. Maybe I write to allow my natural channel to open.

101. Maybe I write to your beautiful mind, which picks the most vital ideas and strums them along, pulling me into engage.

102. Maybe I write in ascension, rejected by the dust.

103. Maybe I write when my prayers are ripping at the seams.

104. Maybe I write to be brave and believe in what's coming—believe in what I've set in motion.

105. Maybe I write with the freedom to engage in love, hope, and enthusiasm.

106. Maybe I write to interrogate the ego.

107. Maybe I write as though my soul is fully furnished and aesthetically trim.

108. Maybe I write for all who rode with me through the crusades.

109. Maybe I write to submit my skit of heaven's narrative. Synthetic are the elements.

110. Maybe I write for my soul's dynasty, radiant in traits from above, in the magnitude of a proposed love.

111. Maybe I write to put forth an answer to life's prayer.

112. Maybe I write because I have an idea that if you take time and cut it in half, you will have four endings and two great tales to intersect.

113. Maybe I write for who I am now, which is evident in the piece I wrote last.

114. Maybe I write when I am forced to make a choice …

115. Maybe I write to step out of my own way and let my heart reveal its voice.

116. Maybe I write to relent my thoughts and grow what I know.

117. Maybe I write realizing that any measure of depth carries with it a profound burden if you see it as one.

118. Maybe I write for those who are allowed to see, who are saddled with the obligation to then communicate their vision.

119. Maybe I write to engage in integral play. I plan, collect, internalize, relate, interpret, and then reflect.

120. Maybe I write with the daily demand of skill and attention.

121. Maybe I write with a questioning intensity and confronting dialogue.

122. Maybe I write for the freedom of my love story.

123. Maybe I write to the world in you, my friend.

124. Maybe I write to be the voice that will always make time to answer you. Invest in me.

125. Maybe I write with a recognition to a supernatural intelligence that submits order as eternal, joy as a living, breathing entity, and love as a cumulative energy that imagines our every emotion.

126. Maybe I write on the exact page I was meant to come back to, seeming to have planned this. Clever girl.

127. Maybe I write carrying traits of immortality.

128. Maybe I write with the understanding that we are all here sharing from the great pool of infinite words, and quite often you find that you've heard them somewhere else. Very likely you have. Make something out of it! Give it a go! It's by no mistake that the universe keeps throwing these messages back at you.

129. Maybe I write to the sound of music.

130. Maybe I write feeling as though I've been here before.

131. Maybe I write with the one thing that can never be taken away from me: an education.

132. Maybe I write on a swinging pendulum.

133. Maybe I write to our united retreat, our infinite home.

134. Maybe I write to set sail for freedom, come a clear night sky.

135. Maybe I write with the patience to birth my truth.

136. Maybe I write because I promised a man when he prayed with me in one of my darkest hours that when I resurfaced, I would write the story. He told me, "The story will write itself." True.

137. Maybe I write as quite the flawed specimen.

138. Maybe I write to remember the moment when …

139. Maybe I write to throw away the list of traits that have kept me separated from the herd for so long. This is a time for blending. Time to paint the shell of indifference.

140. Maybe I write as a nomad on a humble homeward cause.

141. Maybe I write to capture a memory and pull it out from within the filing cabinets of my mind.

142. Maybe I write to know balance and harmony.

143. Maybe I write to remind myself that I will always be known, so long as I always have something to craft.

144. Maybe I write to erase the rewind, live on play, and rest with pause.

145. Maybe I write because being a thinker is not enough, and not enough is a nasty habit to form.

146. Maybe I write for your smile.

147. Maybe I write to cross swords with the very physicality of penmanship.

148. Maybe I write to catch the day it all started.

149. Maybe I write to the audience in my mind—all the carefree stowaways.

150. Maybe I write to garden my mentality.

151. Maybe I write to embody a prized achievement.

152. Maybe I write to discipline my character and commit.

153. Maybe I write with loyalty and motivation.

154. Maybe I write to get as much out as I can before I get off at the next exit.

155. Maybe I write determined to use every available minute in this mode to my advantage.

156. Maybe I write to place an order on my visualizations.

157. Maybe I write to paint a picture of what I'm reaching for.

158. Maybe I write to help you get to where you want to go, to see you successful, and to measure a degree of my success off of that.

159. Maybe I write to greet you first.

160. Maybe I write to enter into a marketplace where fresh produce of thought is always available, for a reasonable price.

161. Maybe I write because you never know when a few words from the heart will spark joy in another's life, and have a lasting impact.

162. Maybe I write to make room for new information and crisp ideas.

163. Maybe I write as some see it unconventional and thus critique. I'd critique myself for conforming.

164. Maybe I write carrying an optimistic working attitude—something I've always catered.

165. Maybe I write to turn off the television, shut down the Internet, and put down the books. Time to layout a serene foundation for productive work.

166. Maybe I write to receive a degree in aptitude and vocation.

167. Maybe I write because I've always said, "The greatest teachers I've had in life are the ones who never retire their role as a student, who are constantly looking to learn from their pupils."

168. Maybe I write as I am always looking to enhance a skill by applying it earnestly.

169. Maybe I write because I find the aspirations of others to be quite marvelous.

170. Maybe I write to find a happy medium.

171. Maybe I write to see the theme forming in this life.

172. Maybe I write in hopes to meet someone who is ready to gamble with something completely new. Gamble to play. Play to win.

173. Maybe I write to speak now the truth I was once unable to comprehend.

174. Maybe I write to always be in good company.

175. Maybe I write to detect any subtle change in mood or circumstance.

176. Maybe I write like rolling dice. I do not know the outcome in advance.

177. Maybe I write knowing reality is created by the spectator.

178. Maybe I write set to wake up before the crew, to unite us all in some way, and string along the story of our journey till our ship reaches its final destination.

179. Maybe I write to have something to travel back to, introducing a personal paradox.

180. Maybe I write as the protagonist of a reality parallel to our world.

181. Maybe I write to set up an alternative branch in the present, one in which I find I never existed.

182. Maybe I write to split a feeling and emotion that once stemmed from a correspondence.

183. Maybe I write a footnote in a vast expanding series.

184. Maybe I write as it is the greatest of all my instincts, in that it allows me to be playful.

185. Maybe I write to give myself something to say, "All right, let's have another look, shall we?" to.

186. Maybe I write as a part of a team of innovators, revolutionaries, and leaders of the twenty-first century.

187. Maybe I write because it is as vital to my life force as carbon is to oxygen.

188. Maybe I write to throw my dreams up into the hands of the universe, never knowing what may show up at my doorstep.

189. Maybe I write to build for myself the world I want to live in.

190. Maybe I write to know life through the adversity of my fellow dreamers.

191. Maybe I write because I do not blindly tread into battle without a sound course of action.

192. Maybe I write to know freedom in my limited possessions.

193. Maybe I write as the seed to do so was planted in me at birth. It came with instructions.

194. Maybe I write to comfort myself in a way a lover seeks to comfort me—a sacred intimacy.

195. Maybe I write for the possibility that I will not be the one to finish my story.

196. Maybe I write no longer ashamed of being the last one to finish. My power comes from being the first one to start.

197. Maybe I write for the one who left me questioning, daring to fall.

198. Maybe I write knowing that the beauty of my story is in the fact that no one ever let me fail.

199. Maybe I write because my desire has never been to be the best, just to be better than my last best.

200. Maybe I write to go back and retrace the history written in the lines of one's face.

201. Maybe I write to pluck the most peculiar, precious word.

202. Maybe I write to speak a personal message I wrote as a gentle reminder: "If you fail today, stop. For today, for just a moment, smile at yourself. Laugh and create a new moment that fits you and all you deserve."

203. Maybe I write for both the pain and pleasure I witness without flinching, without grasping or avoiding.

204. Maybe I write with the key to a kingdom under the wayward sun.

205. Maybe I write until I am rooted in this earth.

206. Maybe I write bold in spirit but patient in heart.

207. Maybe I write as a timeless work of art, bound in individuality.

208. Maybe I write to exacerbate my confusion, becoming my own beloved jester to my kingly court; still my conscience feeds only on the scraps from my soul's table, never allowed to sit equally with the other parts, knights at a long, rectangular buffet whose hierarchy flickers in the shade of many torches.

209. Maybe I write for the first day of my real life.

210. Maybe I write in a time of praise, with the empowerment and salvation of grace.

211. Maybe I write on a road of peace, laced with heavenly adornments.

212. Maybe I write to refrain the fight and invite the pension.

213. Maybe I write to transfigure mere words into gleaming personal treasure.

214. Maybe I write of a fate that paints the way in gold.

215. Maybe I write for the nature of the mystery—a mystery that is legend to my history.

216. Maybe I write as part of a flamboyant parade, in a warped tour.

217. Maybe I write bound to nothing and free to everything.

218. Maybe I write elected by the most unifying perspective, self-love.

219. Maybe I write to foretell.

220. Maybe I write to relinquish the quest of the all-knowing and share in the vast gift of an expendable intelligence.

221. Maybe I write with a pinky promise that's deeper than blood.

222. Maybe I write because even if our time together is brief, the bond is forged and unbreakable.

223. Maybe I write to take at the least and dream at the best.

224. Maybe I write to give beyond what is gifted.

225. Maybe I write for the wish I made when I blew out my first candle.

226. Maybe I write to go the distance.

227. Maybe I write as my identity becomes less abstract.

228. Maybe I write to plunge my imagination into the most obscene of possibilities.

229. Maybe I write because it is a gift that cannot be regifted.

230. Maybe I write to be the closest today that I have ever come.

231. Maybe I write because my heritage is as sacred as my destiny.

232. Maybe I write to know my own depth.

233. Maybe I write to reveal a multitude of emotion.

234. Maybe I write to peel back the tapestry that covers the void.

235. Maybe I write notoriously clever—cleverly notorious.

236. Maybe I write to resurrect and revolutionize the way art is imagined.

237. Maybe I write because this is my year to celebrate how far I've come.

238. Maybe I write with courage to wage, loving the madness.

239. Maybe I write to invest my time and energy where I see good fortune and a profound difference being made.

240. Maybe I write in conjunction with a refined form, with infinite possibilities and period-less propositions.

241. Maybe I write for the reflection that lies within this line of work.

242. Maybe I write apart from the delusion of man, who feels with his eyes and denies the taste of satisfaction, living in a kingdom of dust, made man, made stone.

243. Maybe I write because everything I've ever done, somehow I've wanted to do.

244. Maybe I write believing spirit is purely matter.

245. Maybe I write grateful for the learning opportunity that is presented to me.

246. Maybe I write to never give up on something that has worked so hard to keep up with me.

247. Maybe I write expecting great things from the now and the years to come.

248. Maybe I write because it's never too late to change direction.

249. Maybe I write to a waking reality that is in my mind becoming less and less of a secret.

250. Maybe I write for the dream that will be won.

251. Maybe I write to prepare for a life of abundance, health, and harmony.

252. Maybe I write for the magnificent something out there conspiring on my behalf.

253. Maybe I write to detach from self-sabotaging beliefs that are limiting and vexatious to the soul, distractions on my finest path.

254. Maybe I write to one day introduce an explanation for the biochemical shifts that have for so long governed my mind.

255. Maybe I write as the act is just a beaten metaphor.

256. Maybe I write to say something new, something I believe to be true.

257. Maybe I write out of a kind nature, with a smile, to encourage and spread compassion.

258. Maybe I write because there is no use in being impatient. Every great creation comes with time and careful dedication.

259. Maybe I write from a perspective outside my own, graced by the wisdom and insight of an outsider.

260. Maybe I write because I know that what I want is waiting for me, just around the riverbend.

261. Maybe I write learning that when I race through experiences, acting as if I'm on a time crunch, urged to produce answers for the unseen, that I rush through the steps I need to draft the actual assignment.

262. Maybe I write looking back and remembering what life was like and how grateful I am for the sun that set on that time, for I am now in a more fruitful season.

263. Maybe I write for the mysteries of inspiration.

264. Maybe I write because I love to fish around for new ideas and new literature.

265. Maybe I write for a grand high-five.

266. Maybe I write because I have no need to pretend. This is what I'm made of.

267. Maybe I write meditating on the transcendental.

268. Maybe I write to try hard without trying too hard, careful not to surrender too much of my personal power.

269. Maybe I write forever capable of true brilliance.

270. Maybe I write to connect all the dots I scattered about my existence.

271. Maybe I write to remind myself where most of my joy comes from.

272. Maybe I write to quiet the mind and tame the emotions that cradle the flame.

273. Maybe I write despite any disturbance in the force.

274. Maybe I write understanding that my voice is one of so many contributing to empower a multitude.

275. Maybe I write as a vessel of light in this world. Let's shake hands.

276. Maybe I write because I love what I seek and cherish where I've been. Somewhere in the vast expansion of my mind, I've seen what I am to become.

277. Maybe I write to play the part that is casted blindly, by the whim of the source. The decision is serendipitous.

278. Maybe I write to push through feelings of defeat.

279. Maybe I write to jumble up all that I've read before, and rearrange a new order of intrigue.

280. Maybe I write to stay focused on the best of end results.

281. Maybe I write to work at my own forward pace.

282. Maybe I write with the gust to survive.

283. Maybe I write because I trust in my valiant efforts.

284. Maybe I write because many of the answers I seek do not come with rational explanations.

285. Maybe I write to outgrow any faulty dispositions.

286. Maybe I write to play with the facts and inherit the fiction.

287. Maybe I write to rekindle a sacred quality.

288. Maybe I write in the epidemic of a fleeting democracy.

289. Maybe I write because writing is truly therapeutic.

290. Maybe I write to look back in optimum appreciation.

291. Maybe I write to play with all I have idolized.

292. Maybe I write because I am not a machine that operates on command.

293. Maybe I write for the life of my inner child.

294. Maybe I write for the divine order that is present in the chaos.

295. Maybe I write picking among the greatest of attributes on the tree of humanity.

296. Maybe I write for the foundation of truth and a consciousness that is in a constant cycle of rebirth.

297. Maybe I write putting aside my fears on creativity. Creativity is a path for the brave.

298. Maybe I write for my vision to become clear and awaken me.

299. Maybe I write to be an organism distinct from a capitol.

300. Maybe I write to demonstrate a developmental pattern.

301. Maybe I write because part of me lives for the fantasy.

302. Maybe I write to document the voyage, as I'm just streaming along the blueprints now, with as much time as I need to prepare before we set sail. Keep busy every day, not just your days in the sun.

303. Maybe I write to demonstrate a pattern of allegiance.

304. Maybe I write to hit the repeat button on myself, until I learn what is meant for me.

305. Maybe I write to labor and be worthy of what I acquire.

306. Maybe I write to make room for some fantastic idea to surface.

307. Maybe I write to take a backseat with desire, to work on the prayer.

308. Maybe I write because I have much to filter.

309. Maybe I write a story close to my heart, where we both, in theory, fall in love.

310. Maybe I write in trust of my mind to carry out the messages, as I trust my body to carry out its vital functions.

311. Maybe I write as a devotional offering.

312. Maybe I write to have a sense of detachment from the world, but by no means do I mean alone.

313. Maybe I write as the disciple, the student, the passenger.

314. Maybe I write because it is a spontaneous process, practically involuntary.

315. Maybe I write to instill a feeling in you that was once instilled in me.

316. Maybe I write because I am bound to arrive someplace spectacular.

317. Maybe I write, as it is the purest form of intimacy.

318. Maybe I write because some habits are not interchangeable.

319. Maybe I write to tolerate the tension.

320. Maybe I write to release my sense of self, to shift the power source.

321. Maybe I write upon right belief, right dogmas, right action.

322. Maybe I write as I am saved by faith, not the sum of works.

323. Maybe I write like I'm standing on a football field with my higher self and we are shooting fireworks at one another.

324. Maybe I write on a scattered vibration, bending time like a tesseract.

325. Maybe I write to listen to what interests you, to love what brings you joy, and to digest what you teach.

326. Maybe I write playfully in the tug of give and take.

327. Maybe I write with a pinch of salt.

328. Maybe I write to simplify the need for explanations. I do not enjoy being caught up in them.

329. Maybe I write so my spiritual instruction cannot be exploited.

330. Maybe I write for those who will pick this up and say, "Ah, that was handy," or "Hmm, this is fresh."

331. Maybe I write independent from an ungendered power source.

332. Maybe I write to see where I am, instead of where I'm not.

333. Maybe I write to go beyond solving problems that are just a hassling stimulus.

334. Maybe I write as something sensory and automatic.

335. Maybe I write with all that I harness as a connected spirit, with great will, passion, and vigor to conquer, the potential behind utilizing everything that we can become.

336. Maybe I write because this is my idea of unity, trinity with God.

337. Maybe I write because it is a colorful occupation.

338. Maybe I write to emit a new frequency, electing new thoughts, choosing what to release into my external reality, and working as a transmission tower, at the source.

339. Maybe I write because I see it all in code, with each word symbolizing a piece of time, a riddle that rests within the subconscious.

340. Maybe I write based on calculated choices, enforced morality.

341. Maybe I write permitting distractions.

342. Maybe I write keeping in mind that for a dreamer who is a doer, there is no limit to what we can create.

343. Maybe I write to come back to something, and learn to appreciate it—360.

344. Maybe I write to bodies that are fixed and heads that are mirages.

345. Maybe I write to be cast in my own leading role by the Author.

346. Maybe I write to cherish every sunrise, and to be like my mentor told me to be, "the early bird to get the worm." Only I take my time to carefully choose the worm …

347. Maybe I write to drive the cares away.

348. Maybe I write with the thought in mind, *Sometimes the greatest love comes after we've made the greatest mistakes.*

349. Maybe I write for those who have acted as northern stars, guides on my way to you.

350. Maybe I write to add to the bounty of my story, a glorious morning.

351. Maybe I write for the one who wished my dreams so sweet, whose fateful perspective I took to rest.

352. Maybe I write for a friendly universe, where I've saved a patch of its shade to share with you.

353. Maybe I write, for it is a science that trends practically.

354. Maybe I write best knowing you are only a thought away. Being with you in the glory of the mind is salvation.

355. Maybe I write in adoration of the upswing of your well-being.

356. Maybe I write claiming the life that is mine alone, a life of self-love, which is all I have left to claim.

357. Maybe I write to be involved in something I cannot yet articulate with certainty, or state yet what I think it is.

358. Maybe I write on a pace that is best for everyone, an order we are all cycling through.

359. Maybe I write to fall in love with you each and every day.

360. Maybe I write with a thought "to be remembered," and then I step out into the light and say, "I've already achieved that."

361. Maybe I write to free the final word.

362. Maybe I write for the layers of life behind each tattoo.

363. Maybe I write unable to break away to see that identity is a strong lie.

364. Maybe I write with a given inch, for with it I can draw out a map and place a marker one inch closer to you.

365. Maybe I write to overcome any shadow of illness that sought to cloud my mind.

366. Maybe I write as a caring tenant. I have tidied up my space. When you come to collect your due, I will have left you with an advance.

367. Maybe I write to find humor and to produce humor. My grandmother tells me that if I am to write, I must lighten up my depth every now and then and be silly. I find the things in life that are most unforgettable are the ones that give us a reason to have a good laugh. Sometimes just in the "aha" of the moment.

368. Maybe I write for Tuesday.

369. Maybe I write for the peace that comes with every pause.

370. Maybe I write to hold you close, to back you in the struggle.

371. Maybe I write for all those who have given me a story to carry in our brief but memorable encounters.

372. Maybe I write for my father, who reminds me that there is no such word as *can't*.

373. Maybe I write to create a passage, a wormhole, a paradox.

374. Maybe I write with the help of my little house elf.

375. Maybe I write purely because I crave a new perspective, a new take.

376. Maybe I write for the patterns of divinity.

377. Maybe I write in moments of decision that shape the error or grace of my being.

378. Maybe I write while pairing two variables, energy and time.

379. Maybe I write to experiment with and play on words, which I use to make sense of everyday life.

380. Maybe I write with the privilege to communicate.

381. Maybe I write with the ethereal rhythms of day and night.

382. Maybe I write to act as a midwife of inspiration for another who is in the spotlight to endure the birth!

383. Maybe I write with the freedom to express my creative nature and have it reflected back to me in your response.

384. Maybe I write because I know that if I was to get close to you, I would be entering into a strapping course of enlightenment.

385. Maybe I write so one day someone can pick up where I left off.

386. Maybe I write facing humanity, and realistic fears, learning that I am not alone to face them.

387. Maybe I write with a glittering, pixilated imagination.

388. Maybe I write to move beyond limitations once perceived to be set by the world around me.

389. Maybe I write out of the deepest affinity for someone who cares to enlighten me in the most intellectual of conversations.

390. Maybe I write to connect to my internal world, reminding myself the blueprint for these internal feats has already been drawn out.

391. Maybe I write to get closer to the people and places that help me come alive.

392. Maybe I write in light of the serenity prayer, given the courage to seek change in what I can, and have the wisdom to know some things I cannot.

393. Maybe I write to walk on the water of my imagination.

394. Maybe I write from the point of view of the master looking upon the creation, feeling all that creation feels, and responding in accordance to the relation, not the grounds of the relationship.

395. Maybe I write in light of John 3:15, "We speak of what we know and testify of what we have seen." This is my testimony.

396. Maybe I write from the pool of wisdom that has been passed down through the generations.

397. Maybe I write to give myself a break from the mundane.

398. Maybe I write in practice of Phowa, the transference of consciousness for Tibetan Buddhists, performed for the passing.

399. Maybe I write with the power of the healing stones I set under my pillow each night and set by my side when I work.

400. Maybe I write remembering that I live in a dream world, the universe tells me, where tomorrow everything can drastically change for the better.

401. Maybe I write peeling back at the sum of a question. Answers often have layers.

402. Maybe I write to stop pretending that this world is sane, for right before your eyes, lives are traded in for numbers in some crowned man's game.

403. Maybe I write, working for a future where nothing is ensured but many tools are given.

404. Maybe I write to make out free, and make my mark. For though we are told our maker is pure, can we make out with the purest heart?

405. Maybe I write feeling fed these words, as they come free. Whatever be their origin, I know they are signaling me.

406. Maybe I write because this is the best way to express what I've been visualizing.

407. Maybe I write to know true nobility, wealth in wisdom.

408. Maybe I write to inspire the children, old and young.

409. Maybe I write with a new pair of lenses each time.

410. Maybe I write for all the people who see with their inner eyes the legend in another.

411. Maybe I write for the gracious people, the greener earth, and the clearer day.

412. Maybe I write playing mind games with myself that are as ridiculous as they are intense.

413. Maybe I write pulling from all I have written up to this point, just reimagining it in a new order.

414. Maybe I write counting the times I thought, *Forever.*

415. Maybe I write down the feelings that are confronting me in this moment.

416. Maybe I write to solve with words a pressing conflict.

417. Maybe I write as a lightworker, an indigo child. We activate in order to enlighten.

418. Maybe I write to mold a dream.

419. Maybe I write for the old man in the thrift shop who told me I must keep the spirit of "the Pan."

420. Maybe I write to stay the course, and seek comfort in knowing I have recorded a wonderful life. The time will come to hit replay.

421. Maybe I write for the lesson learned in always trying to prove my self-worth to someone outside myself instead of believing that worth to radiate at its own free will.

422. Maybe I write as the jokester in the tale whose lightheartedness toward any and all outcomes inevitably saves the day from limited thinking.

423. Maybe I write with the true illumination of the stars.

424. Maybe I write to answer your call.

425. Maybe I write to be shown a pretty good time.

426. Maybe I write to turn the gears as the rivers flow and the trees grow.

427. Maybe I write to be awakened by forgiveness.

428. Maybe I write daring you to swim when the storm is coming in.

429. Maybe I write since you came along and passed me the ball.

430. Maybe I write to make something out of the fortune I have found.

431. Maybe I write for the strange things I have to say. Just come a little closer, take a listen, and tell me it's okay.

432. Maybe I write to offset the skeptic and the agnostic who say there is no use pursuing the quest for the great mystery of life. Here I am pursuing.

433. Maybe I write for you, who sees me differently.

434. Maybe I write in a world where we are all young together.

435. Maybe I write kept together by love, the love for the truth in knowledge, love as the desire for self, and love for the motive behind all that is in remission.

436. Maybe I write to one day say, "This was once an idea in a notebook years ago."

437. Maybe I write to create a ticket to the world.

438. Maybe I write to give you the gift of a feeling.

439. Maybe I write with the greatest of wishes to a life where I can fully perceive myself as spirit—to become love.

440. Maybe I write to work outside a stream of Wi-Fi.

441. Maybe I write for an opening experience with a professor my first year in college who gave me an F on a paper I worked night and day to complete. When I came to him in his office hours to ask him to explain why I received the grade, he told me that my paper reminded him of Einstein, that I took the topic outside the box and gave too many metaphors. Einstein found a major energy source in the one place where no one had thought to look. It was hidden in solid matter itself. Perhaps in my out-of-the-box thinking and use of metaphors, I too found a vast energy source. Perhaps it was worth taking a second look …

442. Maybe I write to derail the process of "hows" and "means."

443. Maybe I write to entertain contradictory thoughts.

444. Maybe I write for the happy-go-lucky moments.

445. Maybe I write to put down the habit I picked up.

446. Maybe I write assuming that you already know the truth.

447. Maybe I write in a time of healing, transformation.

448. Maybe I write with the confidence of how well everything works out when you surrender your control to the will of a higher power.

449. Maybe I write looking for a solution in the source.

450. Maybe I write for the flowers that turn their face to the sun.

451. Maybe I write as a gentle reminder to myself that I have a say in my destiny and it's unfolding exactly as I always hoped it would.

452. Maybe I write for this world and all its perspective rules that seem to ignite the most wonderful blessings in disguise.

453. Maybe I write having gone through indignities, but I rose with bravery and perseverance.

454. Maybe I write to accept the responsibility of both my happiness and my unhappiness.

455. Maybe I write to learn the lesson that reality is not what my mere eyes see, but what my mind creates. I am not limited by common logos, pathos, ethos, the past, the unknown future, or the world in which I dwell. I am here to reimagine it.

456. Maybe I write of an innate courage, and I know courage to stretch vast lands and exist in so many. It is to be shared.

457. Maybe I write to put a spin on luck, and say, "Good faith."

458. Maybe I write on the edge of my seat, ready to jump into the next course of action, whatever it may be, at a simple trusted demand.

459. Maybe I write because once when I was a little girl sitting in a little bistro in the Village of New York City, Leonardo DiCaprio came and sat at the table next to me with a man with him, both in all black with black sunglasses. I took the napkin from the restaurant and bucked up the courage to go ask him for his autograph. When I finally got over to speak to him, the man with him looked at me and said, "What took you so long to get over here? You're such a cute girl." He signed for me, "To Rhiannon, 'Best of Luck,' Leonardo DiCaprio." In his note and all throughout my life people have been telling me, "Best of luck" on very unique occasions. Ever since that day when I picked up my pen to write, I would sign it with an artistic signature he inspired me to create.

460. Maybe I write for a father's prayer.

461. Maybe I write reminding myself that every peak must know a fall, and every low must render a rise.

462. Maybe I write without boundary or filter to constrict my creative drive.

463. Maybe I write to draw closer and go deeper into a universal unity.

464. Maybe I write involved in so many stories as a compassionate passerby.

465. Maybe I write because I have always dwelled where the way was lit.

466. Maybe I write to leave a state of exile, by first making peace with the fact that I was there.

467. Maybe I write working with you through the comforts of the mind, to meet you with nothing, just a form that becomes a canvas in your mind as you learn to paint the abstract stranger.

468. Maybe I write to know personal astonishment.

469. Maybe I write to be persistent, guts over fear, the courage to create.

470. Maybe I write, for telling is such that all stories, when given life, become true.

471. Maybe I write for time. Man made time to help God keep track of memories. Time was man's gift to God, and with it, God was able to stop playing, to press pause, to rest.

472. Maybe I write to do more than run, grow and nourish my vessel of light, but to embody a unique, ever free-willed soul, learning the maze of the mind.

473. Maybe I write because I comprehend the blessing of simplicity, of silent gospel, of music that is of no sound, but of waves and shape.

474. Maybe I write as an artist who introduces all works as masterpieces, even in their most fragile states, for they are in a constant state of mastery and reinvention.

475. Maybe I write because I don't want to sit with the hunger. I want to satisfy it.

Printed in the United States
By Bookmasters